A Single Blade of Grass

Also by Ellen Grace O'Brian

Living the Eternal Way:
Spiritual Meaning and Practice for Daily Life

One Heart Opening:
Poems for the Journey of Awakening

The Sanctuary of Belonging

A SINGLE BLADE OF GRASS

OF GRASS

Finding the Sacred in Everyday Life

ELLEN GRACE O'BRIAN

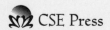 CSE Press

Cover design: John Buse
Book design: Jason Gray
Cover photograph from Photodisc/Photolink
Photograph of author: Paul Schraub

ISBN Number: 0-9660518-3-1
Library of Congress Catalog Number: 2001093369

Printed in the United States of America.
10 9 8 7 6 5 4 3 2 1
This book is printed on acid-free paper ∞

CSE Press
1146 University Avenue
San Jose, CA 95126
(408) 283-0221
info@CSEcenter.org
www.CSEcenter.org

In memory of my mother,
Helen Olive Nicholson

ACKNOWLEDGEMENTS

Lotus growing in the middle of the lake:
Who can gather it?
Grass growing under our feet:
All are served by it.

—*Rabindranath Tagore*

This book is offered with gratitude to my Mother, to my Heart Teacher, Roy Eugene Davis, and to the enlightened sages, friends, and students who continue to help me become a useful human being.

And I especially thank those whose gifts contributed to making this book useful for others: Paul Kelly, publishing guide and inspiration, writer's counselor, wise soul and good friend who supported the work at every turn; Steve Hall and Kathy Indermill, who combined their steadfast commitment to the message of this book with their technical skills to help love be revealed; Lucille Gagnon, who consistently moved the project forward with love and grace;

Michelle Davis, whose editorial skills and spiritual vision blessed the book; Nancy Newlin, whose copyediting talent and can-do attitude brought a breath of fresh air to the project; John Buse, visionary artist and joy to work with, who captured the heart of the book with his exquisite cover design; Jason Gray, whose inspired layout design made the pages speak; Jeff Nicoll, who translated the spirit of the inspirations into a beautiful ad design; Bob Greenebaum, who supported the quality printing of the book; Judith Cornell, whose encouragement for the book was a blessing; Jan Samson, dear friend whose ongoing walks of support have made all the difference; and the CSE Board and community members who enthusiastically embraced this project.

To my husband Michael, I say thank you for helping me find the sacred in our life together every day.

CONTENTS

INTRODUCTION

*All that a man has here externally in multiplicity is
intrinsically One. Here all blades of grass, wood and stone,
all things are One. This is the deepest depth.*

—*Meister Eckhart*

What is love? The scriptures tell us: God *is* Love. Yet the
only thing most people know about God is that God is a
mystery, beyond the mind's ability to comprehend and the
tongue's ability to speak.

The great teacher Paramahansa Yogananda, who brought
the inspired methods of Kriya Yoga, the science of God-realization, to the United States in the 1920's, taught that the
God of love can be known. As Yogananda said, "He is wis-
est who seeks God. He is the most successful who has found
God." His simple declaration contains the radical wisdom
that is the hallmark of all the great ones. The proverbial
good news is that it is possible to find God. It is possible because we exist in God now, at this moment. The scriptures,
the spiritual teachings, and the enlightened teachers witness

for us what is possible and invite us to experience the mystery for ourselves. That it was possible for them shines a candle of hope before us.

A great amnesia, known as spiritual ignorance, is rampant in our world today. This condition causes us to reject the possibility that we can find God. Spiritual ignorance encourages the kind of thinking that splits the soul apart from God, heaven from earth, and body from mind and soul. It blinds us to what is true—we are the love we seek. Finding God is coming home to the truth of our own divine nature. It is possible to find God because we exist *in* the heart of God. The spiritual way of life is waking up from the amnesia of ignorance to this truth and living by it each day.

How do we seek God? By stopping, looking, and listening. By peering into the darkness of inner stillness and listening to the language of silence. Then we discover that the Mystery is really no mystery at all, that it gladly and graciously reveals Its secrets to sincere and receptive hearts purely desiring truth. This is the great secret the saints are trying to tell us: Choose love. Live by love. Have the courage to claim your inheritance.

Waking up spiritually is like waking up from sleep. First there is an inner urge. An alarm bell goes off. Something happens that causes us to think more deeply about life, to question our beliefs about what is real or important. This alarm is a manifestation of God's grace, that aspect of Divine Consciousness that is consciously striving to bring all souls back to Itself. With the support of God's grace, our own efforts are quickened and we find it possible to persevere on the path. This is how spirituality evolves from possibility to actuality.

The spiritual path is universal because God is universal. It is not the possession of any one religion, vocation, class, or race. While there are infinite ways of living the awakened life, there are two key elements you will find in any true spiritual life: first, the primacy of one's relationship with the divine Self or God; and, second, a virtuous way of living in the world. Although there is no causal relationship between moral behavior and enlightenment, there is a correlation. Enlightenment always supports right action, though one cannot "buy" God just by being good.

Because enlightenment is our true nature, you would

think it should be possible to achieve it now, instantly. Nevertheless, in most cases, it is a matter of gradual awakening. It takes time. During the interval, spiritual teachings help support the striving devotee, acting as a hedge to keep out the intruding weeds of doubt and lethargy. Otherwise, following our initial wake up call or glimpse of truth, we tend to fall back into our old habits of forgetfulness. Spiritual teachings and spiritual company remind us to put one foot in front of the other, one thought in front of the other, until the goal of God consciousness is attained and the radiance of the divine Self shines unimpeded.

The inspirations in this volume are an offering of encouragement and support for those on the journey of awakening. Most of them appeared originally on a chalkboard in the meditation garden at the Center for Spiritual Enlightenment, an interfaith spiritual center in California. Each day, an inspiration is written on the board for those who come to the garden to pray and meditate. You are likewise invited to make use of these inspirations. Contemplate them one by one, allowing each the opportunity to evoke your own inner wisdom.

Spiritual wisdom is not something that comes from the outside, from a book, or even from a teacher. True wisdom emerges from the well of enlightened knowing within our own consciousness. The presence of a spiritual teacher, or truth teachings, can help us awaken from our slumber and remind us to keep on in our journey to the Self. But we each must make the journey ourselves. Knowing this, Yogananda advised those who desired Self-realization to read a little, meditate more, and think about God all the time.

Many seekers reverse this formula, reading spiritual books as if enough information could bring about an enlightened condition, neglecting meditation or "trying it" with only sporadic efforts and results, and letting the mind be filled with worries instead of thinking about God. This is a sure way to remain a seeker and not a finder! Those who want to find God, undertake the daily divine discipline of looking within.

The four parts of this book are related to four key areas of spiritual practice. "Polish the Gem of Awareness" offers encouragement for prayer and meditation and for establishing a daily practice of divine communion. Part two, "Look

Into the Heart of Truth," invites us to explore our intuitive wisdom and strengthen our spiritual discernment. The third part, "Cultivate a Peaceful Mind and a Good Heart," offers reflections on living a moral life by following universal spiritual values such as harmlessness and truthfulness in our relationship with others and our world. The last part, "Fall in Love with Your Life," is a look at the grace-filled life of surrender.

These four areas of practice—meditation, contemplation, cultivation of the virtues, and surrender—offer a balanced approach to finding God. Balance is the safest and quickest way to divine realization. Those who attempt to cultivate a virtuous life without the benefit of meditation, or who develop great will but neglect cultivating surrender, or who spend all their time meditating without serving others, discover great difficulties on the path. The devotee who consciously cultivates all four areas of practice finds steady progress.

The spiritual life is difficult, but it is simple. What could be simpler than putting God first? It is difficult because we're not in the habit of doing so. It becomes easier when, instead of becoming discouraged about our lack of progress, we simply say to ourselves, "This moment I will think of God." We can all think of God this moment. And since life is a series of such moments, when all our moments are filled with God, then all our life is filled with God.

But even one thought of God requires faith, the ability to look through the unreal to perceive the Real. To look past hatred and see love, to look past separation and see unity, to look past loss and see gain—such are the ways of the spiritual warrior. Those who choose to live this way have dedicated themselves not only to bringing the light within themselves, but also to calling it forth in the world. This is compassion itself and the highest path of service—living love through acts of compassion and a pure vision of truth.

The spiritual warrior embarks on the journey of awakening with the soul's joy as a guidebook and God as the polestar. These supports help us navigate the maze of choices we encounter each day. Will this choice bring me closer to God? Will it help me to realize my true nature? Does it help others and honor the divinity of all? What will this serve? When our clear intent is God-realization, each day offers steps that can be used as stepping stones toward our goal. To reach the goal requires our sustained, committed participation. And all must be approached with heart. Without love, we cannot find love.

One of the stories from the Hasidic Masters is a tale about a man who goes to the tailor to have a new suit made. The finest fabric is selected with the most elegant design and exquisite buttons to complete the look. The tailor takes the man's measurements and in a matter of days his new suit is ready. When he comes to try it on he is exceedingly pleased. The fit is perfect and the style complements him well. He pays the tailor and walks out of the shop in his new suit. Strolling down the city street, feeling on top of the world in his new suit, he fails to notice one of the seams is loose. It seems that even though tailor had made a beautiful suit, he had neglected to tie the final knot that held it all together. As the man walked along, he began to lose pieces of his fine suit until finally he was left naked!

Spiritual practices, those seemingly small acts we commit to each day, are the threads that tie our life into a meaningful whole. It is no use having a beautiful shell of an outer life if we have not cared for what really matters. A contemporary

Indian saint, Sai Baba, encourages us to "Start the day with love, live the day with love, and end the day with love."

The mystery of love is revealed to us as we live it, as we bear witness to the divine light by letting it shine through our thoughts, words, and actions. Once God is found in the temple of our hearts, we find the divine radiance everywhere. We see the One shining in all eyes, and hear the divine name resounding in every sound. We live, and move, and have our being in joy. We discover that there is a logic to love guiding our every choice that is not the logic of the world. As Cardinal Suhard writes: "To be a witness does not consist in engaging in propaganda, nor even in stirring people up, but in being a living mystery. It means to live in such a way that one's life would not make sense if God did not exist." Be the living mystery of divine love.

May these inspirations help light your way. Read a little each day. Then meditate and experience in divine communion the wellsprings of your own inner wisdom. And live each moment with thoughts of God lighting up your mind and soul.

PART ONE

Polish the Gem of Awareness

*When you were born God brought you so many gifts that you
will never open them all. Love's voice keeps saying,
"Everything I have is yours."*

—Hafiz

What is it to look, really look, at life? To see others with the eyes of love? To live with faith that opens the heart to awe and wonder? Such a vision, the great spiritual traditions tell us, is not only possible but is ours already. It is simply a matter of attention—as simple as watching our own breathing. And just as difficult.

If you have ever stopped a moment to focus on your breath or to sit still before a sunset, you know how easy it is to get distracted. Yet through practice, discipline, and grace, one can learn to achieve at will a state of focused mental alertness, a state where body and mind unite as one laser beam of power and awareness. When attention is focused in meditation, the mental field becomes calm and the light of the soul shines forth. This spiritual light removes our fears, illumines the path of right action, and shows us the way to live with joy.

Because spiritual awareness is a natural state of consciousness, most people have experienced it at some time.

In the quiet beauty of nature or during a heart opening experience such as the birth of a child, one is filled with awe, a sense of peace, pure clarity, and a realization of our connection with all that is. We remember these moments for the rest of our lives.

Meditation practice allows us to have that divine experience—not just in peak moments, but every day. Meditation is "polishing the gem" of spiritual wisdom. It is the effort we make to dwell in the Self, to rest in our true nature as a conscious being. Meditation is different from dreams, visions, or sleep. It is a heightened form of consciousness in which the body is relaxed, the mind is clear, and attention is anchored in the pure aspect of our deepest Self.

There are four steps to practicing meditation: establish a conducive environment both within and without; practice a technique such as watching the breath or repeating a mantra in order to focus the attention on a single point; surrender, by letting go into the peak experience of meditative awareness; and finally, consciously bring the attention back to mind and body with a sense of appreciation and renewal.

It is helpful to set aside a regular time and place for meditation. If you are able to devote an area of your home for daily practice, the energy of your devotion will permeate the space and positively influence your sessions. Because meditation provides such a wonderful sense of clarity and perspective, it is helpful to begin your morning, first thing, with meditation before becoming involved with the concerns of the day.

When the saint Ramana Maharshi was asked about the best posture for meditation he replied that it is the posture in which the mind is still. Meditation can be practiced seated on the floor, on a cushion, or in a chair. The posture should be relaxed but firm, with the spinal column straight. This posture reflects the quality of mind that is most conducive to meditative awareness—a firm intention to experience God balanced with peaceful surrender to God's grace and timing.

Begin meditation by closing your eyes and drawing your attention within. Offer a prayer of attunement, acknowledging the presence of God, the saints and sages, the divine nature of all beings, and the spiritual nature of your own soul. Most importantly, *feel* your connection to God and to all of life. Inwardly walk through the chapel door of God's omnipresence and experience yourself praying "in" God rather than "to" God. Know that God is nearer than your heartbeat, the essence of your being.

Inwardly direct your gaze toward the spiritual eye, the point between the eyebrows. Focus awareness on your breath, noticing the experience of inhalation and exhalation. Whenever you become involved in thoughts, gently return your attention to the breath. After a while, breathing slows down and becomes shallow, thought activity decreases, and moments of calm, pure, awareness are revealed.

As the experience of peace deepens, let go of watching the breath and rest in meditative awareness. When the attention wanders to thoughts again, you can return to the breath, or begin to conclude your meditation by bringing awareness back to body and mind. Before getting up, make a conscious effort to deeply feel the peace you have gathered within. You are that. Feel that you are refreshed, renewed, and ready to start your day with peace as your companion. Pray for others and the world. Consciously affirm the graceful unfolding of divine purpose and the highest good for all.

As you perform your activities, carry the effects of meditation with you and return to the awareness of the divine presence throughout the day.

Approach meditation with enthusiasm balanced by surrender. Learn to be unattached to whatever results come, or don't come. Accept each sitting for what it is without criticism or judgment. Let it be your offering to God. It will be returned to you when you least expect it, as sudden joy, moments of intuitive insight, and an ever-increasing calmness, especially during times of turbulence and change. The best place to look for progress in meditation is in your life itself. Like the graceful dawning of the sun's light on a new day, the soul's influence, released in prayer and meditation, illumines the landscape of our experience. Who we truly are and what matters most become apparent in that light.

Many traditions tell the story of a traveler who journeys to a far land in search of wealth and wisdom only to find that the real treasure was waiting at home all along. Most of us spend our days in search of pleasure, possessions, and successful careers only to wake up one day disillusioned with it all. With the practice of meditation, we attain happiness and security where it can be found—in the stillness of the soul, right now. Consider the invitation from the *Adi Granth*: "As fragrance dwells in a flower, and reflection in a mirror; so does God dwell inside everything; seek Him, therefore, in your heart." Don't wait. This moment is overflowing with grace.

Be attentive to the divine ache of
the soul that longs for God
throughout your day. Then you
will be ready when the Divine One
comes to you through a kind word,
the beauty of nature, a moment of
insight, or a synchronous event.
The fire of Spirit burns in ordinary
moments.

Look beyond what you see with
your eyes and peer into the day
with your heart. Sense the soul's
presence and experience it
resounding in all that is. Enter the
day like a child willing to play and
wonder. Be yourself without worry.

We discover the spiritual law of
our life by being completely present where we are—with our
family, work, and spiritual practice.
Sometimes there is an expectation
that our spiritual purpose or duty
will be more significant or
glamorous than our life is now. But
God is no more present in one
place than in another.

Observe the nature of thoughts as
they move through your mental
field. They rise like waves, powered
by the energy of association and
memory. Watch. Then rest consciously in the peaceful interim
before another wave appears.

To turn the mind from fascination
with material objects, cultivate the
awareness of joy—unconditional
joy, all-pervading joy, steady joy,
peaceful joy. Joy is the one quality
that permeates all of life. Ego is the
"I maker." Soul is the opportunity
maker. The opportunity to experience infinite good and divine joy
exists in every moment.

One conscious breath can change
your life.

When we desire something, we are often unwilling to ask for soul guidance, lest it differ from the ego's plan. But learning to listen deeply to the soul is essential on the path of awakening. Do not be influenced by desires or look to others to establish right conduct. Look within.

Confusion occurs when ego is in
conflict with the soul. The secret
of secrets will not be revealed so
long as the heart is hardened by
self-hatred or contempt for the
spiritual life. Clarity comes when
we open our heart and surrender
to the goodness of the higher Self.
Peace is the calling card of true
inner guidance.

The gifts of soul-inspired intuition
are meant to be put into action.
Each time we trust our intuition,
we strengthen our faith. Following
God's word draws us near to God.

To receive guidance, cultivate a quiet mind. Silence self-serving desires to light God's all-illuminating lamp of wisdom.

Comparing oneself to others is like
driving down a road trying to
follow a map from another city.

Attachment to the teacher is an
obstacle on the path of awakening.
The teacher is a boat that carries
us across the turbulent river of
spiritual immaturity and mistaken
beliefs. When we reach the other
shore—with realization of our
own divinity and the responsibility
it entails—we then rely on inner
wisdom to guide us.

To dwell in silence is to drink from the holy well, to be renewed by the living water of Spirit. Drinking from the soul's well each day yields satisfaction and contentment. People spend almost all their time trying to fulfill desires and needs. But time spent in prayer and meditation cultivates an inner magnetism that draws whatever we need.

Don't look for solutions to
problems in meditation. Rest in
that state beyond problems, where
only divine harmony exists. Divine
guidance will emerge from that consciousness. Bring light into a dark
room, and the darkness vanishes as
though it had never been.

The light of the soul is revealed in
stillness. When the roving senses,
active mind, and dividing intellect
cease their dance of distraction,
divine sight shows us the way.

Once you are immersed in the
ocean of divine bliss in meditation,
there is no need to jump back onto
the shore of technique.

A continuous dialogue occurs
between soul and Spirit. The sym-
bol of this dialogue is Aum or
Amen, the Holy Word. Listening
for this word brings us into divine
communion. Once heard in meditation, it will comfort you
throughout your day. Listen.

Once you experience divine
communion, there is no going back.
You are either in God-consciousness,
or sweetly haunted by the memory
of that experience. During times of
seeming separation, remember the
sweet taste of truth.

The awareness that *God is* answers all prayers.

God knows what we need before
we ask. So why pray? Because
through prayer, we become receptive to divine grace and divine
guidance. First we turn to prayer.
Then prayer turns us.

Dwell in divine remembrance throughout the day—let people, places, and situations remind you of God's presence. To pray without ceasing is to live in love, and to live in love is to plant seeds for your future happiness.

To pray wholeheartedly, we must
pray without attachment to results.
Be completely willing to follow
divine will. We think we know
what's best, but God answers
prayers in infinite ways. Learn to
let go of outcomes by quieting the
mind and learning to see by the
light of the heart.

There are three types of prayers:
Please help. Where are you?
Thank you.

To develop a prayer life, we must
first value prayer. Appreciation
leads us to recognize the many
"prayer windows" that already
exist in our daily lives. Open just
one and gaze into the infinite presence of God.

Destroy the imaginary division
between prayer and activity. Learn
to dissolve stress and worries by
remembering God while you work.

Prayer begins in the mind, moves
to the heart, and finally to the feet.

Spiritual practice requires continuous course correction. Observing our thoughts and choices reveals the trend of our life. Are we aligning ourselves with peace or chasing after desires; living a life of zeal or succumbing to laziness or depression? This is how spiritual practice becomes practical and real.

A strong desire for liberation
galvanizes consciousness, allowing
the seeker to rein in the senses and
steady the mind and intellect in
preparation for God-communion.
A half-hearted desire cannot mus-
ter the focus needed to overcome
inertia or restlessness. Yearning for
God kindles the fire of liberation.

The awakening of spiritual energy
is like lighting a fire in your home.
It is useful if it is contained and
tended. Then the fire can be used
for cooking or heating the house.
Without the container, it will burn
the house down. Spiritual practice is
the container for awakened energy.

The spiritual path is arduous, like swimming upstream against a strong current. Many times we are dashed against the rocks of doubt and self-will. Yet those who persevere are not unrewarded; when least expected they find serene pools of soothing peace for rest and renewal. Ultimately, the vast reservoir of truth is found.

In the *Bhagavad Gita*, the body is
referred to as a city with nine
gates, the openings that are portals
for sensory experience. For the
harmonious functioning of a city,
there must be a city manager who
knows the plan. The city manager
of the body is the purified ego in
service of the soul.

Waking up from identification
with body and mind takes
patience. Once the alarm bell of
Self-realization goes off, the seeker
drifts in and out of delusion. The
discipline of regular spiritual practice sustains awareness beyond the
initial awakening experience.
When spiritual wisdom ripens,
past deeds drop away like flower
petals before fruit. A new life
begins.

PART TWO

❦

Look Into the Heart of Truth

You are truth itself,
and your grandeur is spread over all the earth.

– Psalm 57

Change is the spice of life, bringing us variety and delight. But too much change can be unsettling, upsetting our balance and fueling insecurity. How do we know what is true and lasting when everything is constantly changing? What can we hold on to for support as we navigate the rushing rapids of life?

The perennial wisdom of the world's great philosophies advises us to look beyond life's ephemeral phenomena to discover that which is real and lasting. The religions have said the same thing. In the Sermon on the Mount, Jesus cautions us against seeking security in material goods, in that which "moth and rust can corrupt." He encourages us to seek first the awareness of God and divine order, promising us that whatever we need will then be provided by higher Consciousness. The teachings of the Buddha also advise: "All things arise and pass away. But the awakened awake forever."

How many of us heed that advice? Instead, we idly dream of someday winning the lottery. Of striking it rich in business or through that timely inheritance. These hankerings represent our yearning to realize the soul's riches, the untapped infinite potential within our own depths. If we realize these treasures now, we will cease dreaming about perishable things. This is the satisfaction of awakened ones through the ages, those who relinquished idle dreams to focus on the imperishable gold of Self-realization. "Everything is changing," Saint Teresa of Avila writes. "God alone is changeless."

If we look deeply into what we desire from life, we find that we want three things. We want to be happy and avoid suffering. We want to live and never die. And we want wisdom, the capacity to be aware and know. These three things the world promises us now, their voices proclaiming in unison, "Here! Here! Buy this! This will make you happy, healthy, wealthy and wise." Because our attention is turned outward, we do not hear the voice of the soul whispering, "Here! Here! It is my nature you are seeking; my bliss you are craving. Seek it here!"

If we analyze our life, we see that most of what we think is "us" cannot be us. Is the body us? No. Because the body we have now is different from the one we had ten or even five years ago. Is the mind us? No. Because our thoughts are also changing, even more than the body is changing. What part of us, then, remains changeless? What was our "original face" before we were born? Contemplating this mystery leads to realization of the unchanging soul within, the truth of our real nature long forgotten in the dance with worldly desires.

Beholding the light of eternal existence shining through the shadow play of impermanence, we see through the ephemeral nature of things and circumstances. We are no longer fooled. This realization changes the course of our life. We now realize beyond a doubt that we are part of God and part of all that is. This discovery that we are, have been, and always will be, divine consciousness Itself is not a thought; it is direct knowing through the faculty of intuition. It is soul knowledge. We may not be able to put it into words, but we know it as surely as we know our own breathing. We can say with the mystic poet Kabir: "Just throw away thoughts of imaginary things, and stand firm in that which you are."

The happiness, security, and wisdom we look for in life are all qualities of the soul. The soul is an emanation of God—we are made in God's image and likeness. Just as the ocean wave carries within it the qualities of the ocean, the soul contains the characteristics of its divine source. God's omnipresence, omnipotence, and omniscience are reflected in each of us as existence, bliss, and awareness. These are the precious gems of unlimited potential within our own consciousness. Once we discover this secret, we are free from chasing after the shadows of the soul's joy reflected in the world. We are free to enjoy what life brings without attachment and aversion. We are released from the constraints of fear and doubt and are free to live in love.

This divine awakening is the destiny of each person. Soul development is none other than the inherent urge of life itself. When we turn toward God with a willingness to learn, grace comes to help us. The door of the divine heart opens from within and whatever is needed for God-realization flows into our lives unheeded. Grace is the conscious intention of Spirit to support the flourishing and prospering of Its expression, the individual soul. In the one life that is God, nothing stands between the soul and its own good. As we cooperate with this truth, we find life conspiring to aid and guide us everywhere. New urges well up within us: What is God's will? How can I serve?

With the opening of the heart also comes the spiritual teacher. The teacher is the archetype of the soul's light of truth dwelling within our heart—a reflection of the inner teacher. God within is that teacher, the true Guru, the dispeller of the darkness of ignorance. Without opening the heart, no amount of outer search or entreaty will bring the teacher forth. But in the light of spiritual willingness, you will find the teacher standing before you. The outer teacher is the mirror by which we see the inner teacher, our own divinity. The love we long for is then ours to give away, as the flower girl at the wedding tosses rose petals before the bride.

How can one pray to the
transcendental, to the allness of
Spirit? Understand that allness
includes the domain of relationship.
It is not confined to it, but
includes it.

God is the sheltering presence—
the source of all good, protection,
and love. Take refuge in That.
Troubles come and go; they are
temporary. Look past them to the
One. Divine remembrance frees us
from fear.

Intuition is the key that unlocks
the wisdom of the scriptures.
God's word resounds in the holy
scriptures but it lives in the heart
of the devotee. When God's word
is revealed in the heart, the scriptures become a living reality.

First we know everything. Then we
know nothing. Finally we just—
know.

To imagine we understand God is like holding up a jar of ocean water and announcing, "This is the ocean!" Thought is not experience; it is merely commentary. Experience is just a window offering us a glimpse of a much vaster reality.

Trying to find security and
happiness in outer conditions is like
tying your raft to a log careening in
the same rapids. Anchor the raft of
your life to the rock of
Self-realization.

Actions are expressions of the forces of nature. Learn to observe these forces without identifying with them. Otherwise we are like the bicyclist who continues to pedal on a downhill slope.

Criticism is the opposite of
compassion. Focusing on a single
aspect of failure causes us to miss
the reality of divine perfection per-
ceived by the wise heart. We all
make many errors along the way
and long for healing. Criticism and
blame only deepen the wounds.
Love heals them.

Love is the mighty ocean of God's
presence. Forgiveness is the river
leading to that ocean.

Both compassion and wisdom are
necessary. Without wisdom,
compassion is sightless, unable to
find a way out of its trouble.
Without compassion, wisdom
becomes isolated and smug. Both
are needed for the complete expression of divine love.

Spiritual friendship is based on
shared values. Shared interests are
secondary. A true friend is one
who nurtures the soul. To help
another materially is useful. To
help another emotionally is
compassionate. To help another
spiritually is love.

Love is all-embracing, all-accepting,
all-knowing, all-forgiving—
wholeness itself. When we love,
we are in God and can embrace life
completely. Nothing needs to
change for blessing to occur.

It isn't the cries that count, or the
laments, demands, and deals we
make with God. Only wisdom and
awareness matter. Accept the truth
that the allness of divine love is
here now. The only thing that
stops us from experiencing it is
ourselves, our thoughts about who
we are. We *are* love.

If you want to love God, love your life.

Like a serene lake reflecting the
light of the moon on a clear night,
the quiet mind reveals our true
divine identity as part of all that is.

We are compelled to action not by some external power, but by the force of our own desires that have taken root in the mind. How powerful they are! Stand guard at the door of your mind. Do not allow harmful thoughts to take root and grow.

Cutting off a particular train of
thought is like pruning a branch
from a tree—the energy must then
seek another path. As dissipating
thoughts are continuously
"pruned" through conscious discrimination, the energy of
Self-realization grows.

Meditation is essential for those
who want to practice selfless
service. Without it, we do not see
the selfish desires that creep into
the mind. Meditation practice
turns the light on in the mind and
allows us to see what comes in.

Consciousness is impartial to attraction or aversion—it registers both as mental imprints. These patterns influence our thoughts and feelings and eventually become lenses through which we see the world. Let go. Forgive. Cleanse your mental spectacles by dissolving the old hurts and angers that continue to haunt the soul. Let in the light of God's unconditional love.

When things always need "doing" there can be no satisfaction. Criticism and judgment rule; the heart is pulled in a million directions. It is for no small reason that the great teachers of all ages advise letting go of attachments and outcomes in order to curb the restless tendency of the mind.

Love is unifying; desire is fragmenting. Sometimes we get our signals crossed and go out in search of happiness through possessions, power, or fame. If we could see through personal desire we would find Love itself calling us home.

A belief that God is separate from us opens the door to doubting the very existence of God. In order to manifest our spiritual destiny, the ego self—that which perceives itself as separate and alone—must discover and follow the Higher Self, or Spirit. In the beginning of one's spiritual journey, these two aspects of the Self seem to be at odds. Ultimately, they are realized as one.

Our essential state is conditionless,
a joy that has no opposite. With
no competition, there can be no
fear. The ego strives for survival;
the soul has no rivals. Ignorance of
our true nature is the root of all
power struggles.

There is no "other." There is only
one. What we believe about
another reflects back to us. In
time, it will manifest outwardly.

The great secret of spiritual
devotion is that there is only one
relationship in life. All others are
expressions of that. We know this
when our hearts are broken open
and our ego covering is removed.
Destroy all fear by fearlessly loving
the One.

All is God. No search for the Divine
will ever reveal It.

Wake up from the mortal dream
and live as an enlightened being.
Don't put it off by imagining it is
not possible for you. Enlightenment
is our natural condition. It is the
revelation of our essential nature,
unimpeded by false identification.
Enlightenment already is.

Regardless of any harmful deeds
we may have done, the true Self
remains unstained. The painful
consequences of our errors may
serve to break our heart open and
allow the true Self to shine the
light of compassion into our life.

Spirituality is not something that is attained. It is not a possession—a thing to add to our many things. Nor is it an answer—a panacea for the struggles and pitfalls of life. Nor is it knowledge that one can learn or unlearn. Spirituality is simply who we are. It is reality. When we slough off all the things we are not, it is spirituality that remains.

What is a mother's true name? We call her with an ordinary word that signifies our relationship to her. The name points to something we cannot put into words. So it is with any name for God.

God is an open door, welcoming all.
Anyone may enter, regardless of the
name they call out at the doorway.
The only requirement is willingness
to leave behind the baggage of
self-will and self-importance. Only
those emptied of self may cross the
threshold.

Restraining one's natural impulses
often seems like trying to push a
boulder uphill. And in the end,
what have we accomplished? Fill
your mind and heart with God and
there won't be room for anything
else.

Humility is the willingness and
commitment to be who we are.
True humility is Self-confidence. It
rests on the conscious awareness
of Truth—knowing one's true Self
as Spirit and relying on that and
that alone.

When the mind is agitated with worry and fear, the darkness of ignorance clouds our wisdom. This is when discernment is needed. Like a sheriff breaking up a fight, discernment asks the participants to quietly step outside. Stepping into the light, a new perspective emerges. We can similarly step outside our present challenges by calling on the spiritual power of intuitive discernment.

The same mind that has earned
the title "monkey," by jumping
from one worry to another while
spewing forth an endless stream of
commentary, can be transformed
into the noblest vehicle of spiritual
awakening.

The life of each soul is dear to
Spirit. Just as the ocean pulls all
waves back to its bosom, God is
actively drawing all souls back to
their divine home. The success of
our spiritual journey is guaranteed.
Live in that confidence, knowing
God is your constant companion
and ever-present guide.

The accomplishments that we think are so important are not necessarily seen that way by God, whose sole aim is our spiritual evolution. God may actually delight more in our failures, which chasten the ego and lead to divine awakening. When the only outcome we desire is spiritual awakening, whatever happens can serve that purpose.

At the core of our being, we are already divine. Spiritual practices do not create this condition; they merely clear away obstacles to that realization.

The guru is the presence of light, the awakened consciousness of unity that dispels the ignorance of seeming separation between the seeker and God. The supreme teacher is Divine Consciousness residing within us. The outer teacher and the teachings are the mirror that the supreme teacher uses to show us this truth.

Though the physical teacher may
fail or disappoint you, God is
always the true teacher. That
Divine Presence will continue to
make Itself known as the heart is
left open. Even the breaking of the
heart in the student-teacher relationship can serve this purpose.
One must be flexible, willing to
bend and even break without giving up or losing heart.

The teacher's grace helps the
seeker discover God's grace. Ultimately, however, it is our own
grace that is required for liberation.
Those who are willing to thrive, to
live their lives to their fullest
potential, invite the activity of
grace in all three of its aspects—as
God, as the teacher, and as their
own true Self.

Spiritual teachings, when embraced
with faith and practiced by the
devotee, are the connecting link
between guru and disciple, or spiritual teacher and student.
Whatever the stage of development, Truth itself will always be
the one true teacher.

We all have an inner pilot light, a
tiny flame of awakened mind,
awaiting the presence of an
enlightened teacher to turn it up.
Then the cooking of ego can begin.

The spiritual teacher provides a
map for the path of awakening, but
the student must make the journey. The ticket for enlightenment
is not transferable.

PART THREE

Cultivate a Peaceful Mind and a Good Heart

Too long I've wandered from place to place,
Seen mountains and seas at vast expense.
Why haven't I stepped two yards from my house,
Opened my eyes and gazed very close
At a drop of dew on a stalk of rice?

—*Rabindranath Tagore*

$\mathcal{W}$e are living in unprecedented times. Quantum leaps in science are changing the way we see the world, while technology is changing the way we live in it. Yet through all this progress, our faculties of understanding and wisdom are lagging behind. We are in need of a radical technology—a spiritual "technology of the heart"—if we are to answer the crucial moral and humanitarian questions we face and meet the challenges that confront us at this unique time in history.

Real change, resulting in the positive transformation of our lives and our world, depends on spiritual awakening—the ability to see clearly with compassion and wisdom. This is not something new. What is new is the unparalleled access we now have to these timeless truths. Spiritual practices once known only to monks, nuns, mystics, and practitioners of yoga, are now readily accessible to anyone seeking God-realization.

A woman once asked Brother Lawrence, the 17th century Carmelite, about her spiritual progress. He answered that her only problem was that she wanted to "go faster than grace." We face that same temptation today—to try to move faster than grace in our world, putting convenience ahead of conscience and personal power ahead of prayer. With all the information available, there is the tendency to be fooled by the romantic fantasy of an easy and instant spiritual life. But soul advancement is always hard-earned. We may want the "quick fix" but the truth is that nothing replaces daily, patient, spiritual practice as the quickest and most efficient way of hastening a life filled with the grace of Spirit, in tune with God's divine plan.

The most exciting truth is this: Where we are now, God is. While a retreat or spiritual pilgrimage can offer us a temporary change, real progress comes at home, in the "practice hall" of family, work, and community life, where we can get busy with the serious work of freeing the soul from the bondage of the ego. While it would certainly be a relief to escape some of the difficult interactions we have with others, it is often those very experiences that are the most spiritually beneficial. By revealing to us the deceptive tactics of our ego-motivated behavior, such experiences force us to surrender, opening us to an experience of oneness. The illusion of having a separate existence falls away, and the light of the truth shines in our souls. Goodness, compassion, unconditional love, peace, forgiveness, generosity, creativity, dignity, loving kindness, serenity, sweetness, joy, power, wisdom—these qualities of God, and more, express themselves in the human personality made radiant with surrender.

When Confucius was asked, "Is there one word that can serve as a principle of conduct for life?" he replied, "Reciprocity: Do not do to others what you do not want them to do to you." We find this in the Torah as well: "You shall love your neighbor as yourself." And it is reinforced by Jesus saying: "Treat others as you would like them to treat you." Hinduism's Mahabharata says: "One should not behave towards others in a way which is disagreeable to oneself. This is the essence of morality."

The universality of the Golden Rule suggests a corresponding metaphysical reality—that there is one life common to us all. As we are now coming to realize this truth on the material level, so we must realize it spiritually. Even though outwardly we seem to be separate from one another, "skin encapsulated egos" as Alan Watts noted, it is time to awaken to the truth of our oneness with Spirit. It is this awakening that lies at the foundation of a "technology of the heart," a technology that can lead us out of the confusion of these contradictory times into the light of a new era of conscious living.

One day a holy man was sitting near a riverbank when a scorpion fell into the water. The saint reached in to save the drowning scorpion. As he lifted it out of the water, the scorpion stung him. Moments later the scorpion slipped back into the water. Without hesitation, the holy man reached in again to rescue the creature. A young man standing nearby saw all this. He approached the saint and asked, "Why would you pull this scorpion out again when it stung you the first time?" The holy man replied, "It is the nature of the scorpion to sting. It is my nature to help."

A natural, unforced self-discipline is the fruit of spiritual vision. When we truly understand that what we do to others—other people, other forms of life, our own planet—we do to ourselves, we will naturally and spontaneously act rightly. We won't need to read a book for motivation. Neither will we feel we must *work* for spirituality or *try* to become enlightened. We will simply *know* we are spiritual beings *now*. There is nothing to add, nothing to attain, nothing to prove, or gain. We choose to live a virtuous life because that is who we are. We speak, serve, and live the truth because it is our nature to do so.

Most people think being free means doing whatever they want. But true freedom is not doing what we want; freedom is being free from those wants. Wants multiply. The more we have, the more we want, until eventually we become enslaved. Freedom comes from experiencing in meditation the unconditional contentment of the soul, which is ours now regardless of circumstances. Paramahansa Yogananda is one who knew this freedom. He wrote: "Whenever your mind wanders in the maze of myriad worldly thoughts, patiently lead it back to remembrance of the indwelling Lord. In time you will find Him ever with you—a God who talks with you in your own language, a God whose face peeps at you from every flower and shrub and blade of grass. Then you shall say: 'I am free! I am clothed in the gossamer of Spirit; I fly from earth to heaven on wings of light.' And what joy will consume your being!"

The spiritual warrior is guided by
the bliss of the soul, not the whims
of desire. Fulfillment of desire does
not lead to happiness; it leads to
more desires. Nonattachment and
nongrasping open the door to
freedom and true happiness. Let go.

Look to the root of anger to find
the desire it springs from. Trying
to dissipate anger by venting it is
like blowing dandelion seeds in the
wind. They will take root and
spring up again. Use the trowel of
discrimination and pull out the
root.

There are four keys to spiritually healthy relationships: keep your attention on God; let go of self-will and insistence on being right; practice positive speaking that uplifts; and, remain even-minded in all circumstances.

Like a controlled fire in the forest
clears away the underbrush and
supports healthy tree growth,
restraining self-will burns the ego
but clears the way for divine soul
qualities to express.

Habits can be friends or enemies. They can lead us away from the soul or they can become stepping stones to liberation. Good habits are difficult to form in the beginning, so surround yourself with other devotees of God. The encouragement you receive from such company will build your faith and strengthen your resolve.

Resentment builds a prison,
thought by thought. Forgiveness
tears it down all at once.

Genuine kindness is a great
teacher. It reveals God's presence.

Blame is a by-product of
forgetfulness. To criticize and
blame others diverts us from the
important task of self-improvement.
It also prevents genuine human
relationship, which is possible only
with a compassionate heart.
Dwelling on the faults of others is
an indication that we are not
tending to our own. The only truly
effective work we can do is on
ourselves.

What causes us to react unkindly when someone is angry? Restlessness. When the mind is agitated, we cannot perceive the unity of life. This leads to defending an imaginary separate self. We can free ourselves and others from the shadow play of separation by bringing the light of peace into a tense moment. Seeing ourselves in others turns up the light.

Words spoken with conviction
shape one's life and experience.
Consciously and unconsciously, we
use them everyday to wound or
heal, curse or bless, destroy or
build. Each word is a seed. Planted
in the soil of life, they put energy
into motion, giving form to
thought and motivation to intention. Words are the sacred
manifesting power of God within.
Let them serve love.

The desire to know and serve God
brings us closer to the heart of
truth. Truth is disarming. When it
is embraced, miracles happen.

Truth fills our life with the vibrant
energy of the soul. Truthfulness is
the highway to manifestation.
When we live and speak the truth,
there is no interference between
Spirit and soul, mind and matter.
Without interference, the inherent
creative abilities of the soul manifest freely.

Truth remains ever the same.
There is no *new* spiritual truth,
only the perennial wisdom
repeated again and again in the
idiom of the day for those with
ears to hear.

Imagining ourselves separate from Spirit creates the illusion of con-trol. True seekers reject this ploy of the ego, preferring instead the sweet surrender of a soul united to its Lord.

Following another's idea of
worship is like wearing someone
else's shoes. You'll look fine from
the outside, but inside you won't
be comfortable.

Consciousness of the true Self
neutralizes obstacles. They
become like the grass under an
elephant's feet as he marches
effortlessly through the jungle.
Self-confidence is the result of a life
based on Truth.

As like grows from like, so
abundance grows from abundance.
Plenty grows from thoughts of
plenty, while brooding on lack,
poverty, or limitation attracts the
same. Think of all the good, beautiful, and true things that are in your
life today. Be grateful for these.
Praise and magnify these. Open
yourself to the consciousness of
abundance.

Spiritual prosperity has an element
of renunciation in it. With the
realization that fulfillment comes
from within, the seeker cheerfully
and willingly puts a lid on desires,
knowing that material things are a
pale and often misleading reflection
of soul prosperity. Our greatest
riches are within.

The ego's sense of "I, me, and mine" is a barrier to experiencing the abundant joy of life. With the experience of oneness, we enter heaven. We are free to enjoy this beautiful world as part of heaven when we remember the world belongs to God.

It is the nature of Spirit to give
unconditionally. We are Spirit.
Generosity is the truth of who we
are.

Jealousy arises from selfishness.
When we are surrendered to God,
we see others as partners in the
divine plan designed for everyone's
success. Then, how can we be jeal-
ous? Dedication to the success of
others assures our own.

Patience is trusting God's timing.

Prayer allows us to respond to
situations instead of reacting to
them. Before taking action, pray
and let God lead the way.

When the self-serving ego attempts
to dominate life though partnership
with the senses and desire, then
anger, lust, and greed appear.
When the senses are under the
dominion of the soul-inspired ego,
then anger, lust, and greed lose
their jobs and move to the outskirts
of the city where they wait for the
self-serving ego to put them to work
again. If they return, we know ego
has moved back in with desire.

Attraction to objects of the senses is like a creeping vine. At first it blossoms and appears attractive. But if the vine grows unrestrained, it eventually covers the entire garden and leaves the house uninhabitable.

We imagine freedom to be the
ability to choose what we like over
what we dislike. But that is actually sugarcoated bondage. True
freedom is being free from both
likes and dislikes. When we are no
longer compelled to seek out what
we like and avoid what we dislike,
we are free to follow the soul's
guidance.

Prayer for the workplace: "God be my day planner today. Help me to remember that You call all of the meetings and that all work is for your sake. When I see my coworkers I will think only of You. I will put others first, offering my service at your feet. The workplace will be my practice hall today."

A spiritual life requires us to give up attachment to appearances. You may appear inconsistent, even foolish, while you are growing spiritually. Let the courage of your convictions be the inner light that illuminates the integrity of your character and the purity of your purpose.

Gratitude comes when we let go.
When we cease fighting what is,
the glory of what can be emerges.

Spiritual practice is distinguishing between our wants and our needs—learning to choose what pleases the soul over the passing whims of the ego. Impatience is a form of anger that arises when we do not get what we want. Ask yourself if what you want is more important than peace.

Cease believing that things of the world or outer conditions have the power to help or harm you, and everything will change.

When a desire is satisfied, a temporary calm appears in the mind. We interpret this as happiness. Yet when pleasure from the fulfillment of that desire fades, off we go in search of more. Ultimately, the search becomes exhausting. The joy we access from our own consciousness does not exhaust, nor does it fade. Because it is ours already.

Conscious eating is a sacrament
where food is recognized as a gift
from God to sustain one's body
temple. The energy of the body,
fueled by healthy food, is offered
back to God through selfless
service.

Polish the body with cleansing
practices. Polish the mind with
patience. Polish the heart with
contentment. Then your temple is
ready for the Guest.

Ever-new joy belongs to the one whose heart rests in the Divine. Unconditional joy is our true nature. We do not need to seek it or try to create it. Simply do not allow anything to take it way. The only time joy is possible is now.

Devotional chanting purifies the
heart and mind until only God
remains.

Nothing can shake the person who
has realized God. Circumstances
are only passing clouds in the sky
of pure mind where the light of
truth perpetually shines.

The saints are those who don't let themselves get in God's way.

Cultivating even-mindedness is like planting a garden—it takes time, patience, and dedication. If we allow ourselves to be overcome with anger, it is like pulling out the tender shoots by the root. Patience and contentment are the twin companions of one who would possess God. The seeds planted in this moment are the flowers of our future.

Release the grasping demands of
the ego by resting in the sweet
contentment of inner silence. That
is the way to successful renunciation. To attempt self-denial
without Self-realization is
self-defeating.

Love desires to use us for Its
purposes. Surrender to this truth is
the key to our greatest contentment.

A worried mind lives in the future.
An unhappy mind lives in the past.
Only a peaceful mind abides in the
present. When worry haunts you,
ask: Is it true now? Moods flee in
the light of now.

It is easy to believe we are
even-minded when we are praised.
Our ability to learn from criticism
is more telling. The depth of our
spiritual realization is revealed in
the everyday quality of our
equanimity.

When we have God what can we gain? What can we lose? Things and circumstances are like glass baubles before the immutable gold of Self-realization. They do not unsettle the mind of one anchored in Truth.

PART FOUR

Fall in Love With Your Life

*All things—from Brahma the creator down to a single
blade of grass—are the apparently diverse names
and forms of the one Atman.*

—Shankara

$\mathcal{T}$he spiritual path has been likened to a razor's edge. This scares some people, and they avoid the path, fearing the strenuous effort such an analogy implies. Yet no one can escape, because life itself is the spiritual path. Everyone is traveling this path—whether they realize it or not.

Most people do not wake up until, experiencing deep pain, they look for a way out of that suffering. They look at their lives and realize they cannot, by the force of their own will, create the happiness they are seeking. So they look for another way.

Others don't wait for suffering. They question life. What is truth? Who am I? What is my purpose here? They seek wisdom.

Still others come to the path through love, drawn to self-knowledge through the yearning to love and serve God.

Whatever it is that brings us to that point, once we begin making spiritual effort, we find that we are not alone. To our great delight, we realize that we do not need to make the journey all by ourselves. As soon as we begin making spiritual effort, an inner divine grace meets us to reinforce our endeavors and propel us forward on the path.

The mystic poet Kabir said: "It's the yearning that does all the work." The primary discipline of the spiritual life is to let ourselves be drawn by the soul's natural love for what is life-giving. In other words, to fall in love with our life.

Here is the central paradox of the spiritual path: To become what we already are, and to seek what we already have. Remember when you were a child? You were naturally joyous. How did we lose that joy? We never did. We simply began to identify that joy with external things—our toys and our friends. And then one day all the building blocks fell down and we had nothing.

Or so we thought.

The heart, the seat of the soul, still possesses that joy. The mind may still be consumed with child-like fascination with the toys of this world, but the heart remains ever at home with God. It is the heart that now must train the mind, transform it into a true friend of the soul. The mind that has been seduced by worldly mirages must be redirected within to drink of the inner, living waters of the soul.

The first step is to meditate. The language of the soul is silence. The mind must be taught to sit still in silence. The next step is to carry that peace gathered in meditation into our daily lives. Another word for this is devotion, the realization that in the play of life with its diverse manifestations, there is truly only One with whom we relate—one Spirit, one Consciousness operating behind Its many guises.

When we practice devotion, when the mind returns to thoughts of God during activity, we begin to see something that we have missed before. We notice a shimmering beauty —a vibrant presence transforming the dull grays of a mundane existence into the colors of joy.

For some people, devotion means love for God. For others it is devotion to Truth. In either case it is the commitment that draws the response. Those who have difficulty relating to a personified image of God may find it easier to contemplate the qualities of God, such as peace, truth, or love. Qualities of God contain the presence of God. Concentrating deeply upon love, one feels divine love. Focusing on peace, one experiences the peace of the soul.

Christ talked about the kingdom of heaven. Few people realize that this divine realm extends to the earth plane as well. There is no place we can go where God is not, no situation in our life where divine love is not there to comfort and guide us. God pervades our life and is our life. The direct path to loving God is to begin to love our life by affirming what is. Even in the most difficult situations it is possible to summon the light of goodness through the power of affirmation.

It is human nature to love certain parts of our life and to reject others. But this causes us to miss the blessings that hide behind distressing disguises. With spiritual vision, we open ourselves to the realization of universal goodness— the truth that everything is working together for the fulfillment of divine purpose and our highest happiness. In a heart made whole by surrender, the dark night of grief heralds the dawn of new life. Accepting life in all its aspects opens the door to experiencing the unconditional joy of the soul.

The mind is magnetized by what it loves. When what we love is God, our life reflects God's presence. Brother

Lawrence practiced this to such an extent that whatever he was doing—whether it was working in the kitchen or kneeling in prayer—he experienced the same sweet communion with the Beloved. "I began to live," he said, "as if there were no one in the world but Him and me." His joy grew. So much so, he found it difficult to contain it.

A simple handwritten note, found in the back of an old woman's Bible, reveals the secret for experiencing divine companionship. It read: "Three rules to live by: Live one day at a time. Do one thing at a time. Trust God all the time."

The spiritual life is not an after-life. It is life now, an eternal life with the ever-present God, the supreme Support, Comfort, and Guide with us always, sharing our joys and sorrows, our victories and defeats with a love beyond that of even the most devoted father or mother, closest friend, or dearest beloved.

Krishna, the Divine Presence, speaking to Arjuna, the soul yearning for true happiness, advises: "I am always with all beings; I abandon no one. And however great your inner darkness, you are never separate from me. Let your thoughts flow past you, calmly; keep me near, at every moment; trust me with your life, because I am you, more than you yourself are."

Admitting we cannot do it on our
own is the beginning of the soul's
victory, the willingness of the ego
to step down. Like the inheritance
of the prodigal, a feast of divine
love awaits that decision.

Time is eternal and energy is infinite—when we live in the present moment.

To live prosperously is to vow to grow. The focus of true prosperity is not on having more, burdening the self with additional responsibility and attachments, but on being more—more aware, alive, joyous, and free. That is prosperity.

Those who believe they do not
have enough to give, don't. Those
who feel they have enough to give,
do. To prosper is to stop holding
back the blessing of our life.

Our daily bread is the sustenance
derived from conscious awareness
of the presence of God. We do not
work for a living; we are sustained
by divine love. God is our life.

The essential spiritual law is: Hold to the One. Seek only Truth and see God in all that is. Only then will we recognize the angels of opportunity that are gathered on our doorstep.

Family life is sacred, and when we
honor that sacredness our
relationships grow, thrive, and
prosper. As our spiritual life is
tended, as we focus on and cultivate our love for God, everything
improves. Worship is the way we
live, whether in the temple or in
the kitchen.

Make a pilgrimage today to the
shrine of your heart where God
dwells.

Wisdom and devotion meet in the
heart and become one. Ultimate
knowledge leads to devotion and
true devotion brings wisdom.

To increase peace in life: seek the
silence of meditation, the company
of those who are spiritually awake,
uplifting conversation with others
on the path, and work devoted
to God.

Be like the songbird perched on the
top of the tree whose song fills the
garden. Keep your consciousness
aloft with remembrance of God.
Your words and actions will bless
those around you.

Devotion is divine remembrance. It inspires us to search for God in all things. Open your awareness to the presence of God like a mother searches for her child in a crowd— with strong intention, confidence, and a clear belief that she will find her little one. For her, everything else falls away from awareness. She seeks only her child. That is how we must seek God.

Our duty in life is to fulfill the law
of our own being, to become in
actuality that which now exists as
potential. Let your attention return
again and again to its Source.
Don't get caught up in the drama
and the dream. This life is over in
a twinkling. If you have forgotten
your purpose, you have forgotten
everything. Fulfill your divine
potential.

Life and all its experiences
magnetically draw us towards
God-realization. We have the
freedom to accept or resist that
pull. By cooperating with divine
will, we become partners in the
divine plan for healing and blessing
the world. Choose God so that
God may choose you.

The bird makes a beautiful and
useful nest by gathering discarded
bits found in nature. In God's plan,
the rejected parts of our life may
similarly prove to be useful.
Everyone's past is full of errors that
can be transformed with wisdom
and compassion.

Jesus taught that we would find
him among the poor. The spirit of
the living Christ within is the voice
of conscience urging us towards
compassionate action.

The spiritual plan for our lives is a living plan, requiring moment-to-moment participation. With each step, the next step is revealed. The universe is divinely ordered. It allows us to fulfill our dharma, the law of our own nature, with the very opportunities that are now at hand.

The spiritual duty we are called to
in our life is precise and personal.
It is the perfect environment for
the fulfillment of our destiny even
though we may carry it out imper-
fectly. Imperfection is our growing
edge.

The essence of faith is realizing
that what God wants, we want.

When we pray in secret,
communing with God in the silent
chamber of the soul, God responds
to us openly. Whether through
dreams, synchronicities, or
seemingly ordinary events, God
comes to us through whatever
channel is open at the time.

If you can't believe in yourself,
believe in God, who is your Self.

Rely on Spirit and trust the
fundamental goodness of people.
Omnipresence is God's cloak of
disguise. Faith removes the cloak.

Once the journey of soul recovery
is begun in earnest, Life itself
conspires to support us. It is up to
us to learn to cooperate with it.
For one who is surrendered to
God, a change in consciousness is
inevitable. It comes like the
approaching dawn. There is a long
time in the dark, then slowly,
barely perceptible changes occur
until finally the entire landscape of
our life is illumined.

Praise is the language of faith. It is always possible to look for what is good and call it forth.

When we examine our motives we
usually find some degree of
self-serving in everything we do.
This is why love and grace are so
important. When we do what we
can to remove self-interest and
offer service out of love for God,
then grace, the divine intention
that seeks our awakening, clears
the way.

Grace is inescapable blessing. It is
always present but only revealed to
us when conditions are right.
Grace knows no effort or cost, no
merit or reason. It is the gift of
divine love given freely.

God's grace sustains us, the
teacher's grace opens us to possibility, and our own grace frees us.

Healing comes by letting go of
mental struggle and resting in the
presence of God, here and now.
Too often we chase after things and
fail to notice our own contentment.
Instead of asking God to fix your
life, invite everything to come into
perfect harmony through grace.

Good works lead us to the door of
heaven, but only love and grace
take us through.

When awareness rests in the heart
of divine remembrance, the path of
right action is lit by grace. The
darkness of the error of self-interest
is removed.

Service contributes to the welfare of others, to peace, and to the repair and healing of the world. Any vocation that is contrary to these cannot be right livelihood. When trying to discern your vocation, ask: Who does it benefit? What does it promote? If it serves the whole, bringing more unity and less divisiveness, you are moving in the right direction. Let Love light your way.

To be engaged in what we do and never once forget God is the goal of the seeker. The more we realize we cannot escape God, the easier this becomes. To all appearances, selfless service is like any other ordinary activity, but inside it is completely different. There is no grasping, pushing, or desiring.

A pure action is pure throughout.
The initial intention toward action
is the desire to please God. The
action itself is done only for God,
without attachment to the fruits.
Then it is offered with love.

Selfless service can be identified by: pure intent; the ability to remain even-minded in times of loss or gain, praise or blame; and depth of caring for the means of the work while surrendering the result. One engaged in selfless service is free from worry or anxiety and is able to welcome obstacles as useful resources toward the goal of awakening.

Happiness comes looking for us
when we seek the happiness of
others. It escapes us when we seek
it for self alone. When we serve
without selfish motive, life itself
sees to it that all our right desires
are fulfilled.

No matter what you have been struggling with, remember, the power of Divine Consciousness is greater. Dwell there now, and let healing enter. Nothing is more essential to the spiritual life than surrender. Nothing we can learn, or do, or master will ever take its place. The decision to surrender changes us forever.

Good works abide in nature; only
surrender takes us beyond. No one,
not even the saints, reach enlightenment through action. But action
is necessary. Just do not imagine
yourself to be the doer of the
action—that is the key. Stillness in
activity requires surrender of the
sense of separate self. When there
is no "individual me" one rests in
the heart of God.

Surrender of the sense of separation does not mean extinction of the individual. It means divine action flowing freely without the conflict of self-will. Regardless of outer accomplishments, if our life isn't in harmony with the law of our soul, it cannot be called a success. Success is living in harmony with divine will.

To be surrendered to God means living in the moment open to what life brings. This does not mean we float along in our boat of life without steering toward a specific destination. Our course is charted toward God-realization, and our rudder is service.

It is not what we do or don't do
that makes us worthy, but the
degree of our surrender. Every day
serve with love; give God your all.
Every night release it completely;
turn it over to God. Each day is
new; begin anew. Do not worry; it
is all God.

SELECTED READINGS

Bly, Robert (versions). *The Kabir Book: Forty-Four of the Ecstatic Poems of Kabir.* Boston: Beacon Press, 1977.

Byrom, Thomas (tr.). *The Dhammapada: The Sayings of the Buddha.* New York: Vintage Books, 1976.

Chopra, Deepak. (edited with new English versions), *The Soul in Love: Classic Poems of Ecstasy and Exaltation.* New York: Harmony Books, 2001.

Delaney, John J. (tr.). *The Practice of the Presence of God by Brother Lawrence of the Resurrection.* New York: Image Books, 1977.

Hirshfield, Jane, ed. *Women in Praise of the Sacred: 43 Centuries of Spiritual Poetry by Women.* New York: Harper Collins, 1994.

International Religious Foundation. *World Scripture: A Comparative Anthology of Sacred Texts.* New York: Paragon House Publishers, 1991.

Mitchell, Stephen. *A Book of Psalms: Selected and Adapted from the Hebrew.* New York: HarperCollins, 1993.

————. *The Enlightened Heart: An Anthology of Sacred Poetry.* New York: HarperCollins Publishers, 1989.

Prabhavananda, Swami and Christopher Isherwood, (tr.). *Shankara's Crest Jewel of Discrimination—with A Garland of Questions and Answers.* New York: New American Library, 1970.

Radice, William and Dyson, Ketaki Kushari (tr.). *The One and the Many: Readings From the Work of Rabindranath Tagore.* Calgary, Canada: Bayeux Arts, Inc., 1997.

Yogananda, Paramahansa. *The Law of Success: Using the Power of Spirit to Create Health, Prosperity and Happiness.* Los Angeles: Self-Realization Fellowship, 1944

————. *Sayings of Paramahansa Yogananda.* Los Angeles: Self-Realization Fellowship, 1952.

ABOUT THE AUTHOR

*R*ev. Ellen Grace O'Brian is the founding teacher and Spiritual Director of the Center for Spiritual Enlightenment (CSE), an interfaith ministry with headquarters in San Jose, California. She has been teaching meditation and practical methods for spiritual living for over twenty years. With a background in the tradition of Kriya Yoga and interfaith ministry, her main purpose is to assist seekers with the discovery of their own divine nature and authentic spiritual way of life. Rev. O'Brian also founded the Love in Action School of Ministry, an interfaith seminary. Her teachings are full of the warmth and wisdom of an "everyday mystic"—a spiritual woman living in the world, with a vocation, a family, and the yearning to serve God. To learn more about Rev. O'Brian's work or to schedule a seminar, lecture or retreat for your group, contact CSE.

Rev. O'Brian's books are available through bookstores, or you can contact CSE directly. Audiotapes and CDs of sermon messages are available as well as a video home study course for developing a daily spiritual practice. Spiritual inspirations such as the ones in this book are written each day on the chalkboard in the meditation garden at CSE. These messages are available without cost to e-mail subscribers. To sign up, go to the CSE Web site.

THE CENTER FOR SPIRITUAL ENLIGHTENMENT

The Center for Spiritual Enlightenment (CSE) is an interfaith spiritual center with headquarters in San Jose, California. The spiritual root of CSE's interfaith teaching is the tradition of Kriya Yoga, the science of Self-realization. The teachings of yoga are a nonsectarian spiritual path for seekers of all faiths interested in exploring the mystical path of God-realization. Meditation is practiced as a way of awakening to spiritual Truth, to the direct experience of our true nature.

The message at CSE emphasizes the potential for all people to awaken to Truth, and the importance of living a spiritually conscious life by following the universal ethical precepts of the world's wisdom traditions such as harmlessness, truthfulness, and right use of our life energy. The Center offers many programs including weekly interfaith worship services, meditation retreats, classes in spiritual living, yoga instruction, spiritual education programs for youth, and an interfaith school of ministry.

For information about the Center for Spiritual Enlightenment visit the Web site, *www.CSECenter.org*